Libra

Also by Sally Kirkman

SALLY KIRKMAN

Libra

The Art of Living Well and Finding
Happiness According to Your Star Sign

HODDER

First published in Great Britain in 2018 by Hodder & Stoughton
An Hachette UK company

8

A CIP catalogue record for this title is available from the British Library

Hardback ISBN 978 1 473 67677 0

Typeset in Celeste 11.5/17 pt by Palimpsest Book Production Limited,
Falkirk, Stirlingshire

Printed in the United States of America by LSC Communications

Hodder & Stoughton policy is to use papers that are natural,
renewable and recyclable products and made from wood grown in
sustainable forests. The logging and manufacturing processes are expected
to conform to the environmental regulations of the country of origin.

Hodder & Stoughton Ltd
Carmelite House
50 Victoria Embankment
London EC4Y 0DZ

www.hodder.co.uk

Contents

• • • • •

Introduction

* * * * *

Before computers, books or a shared language, people were fascinated by the movement of the stars and planets. They created stories and myths around them. We know that the Babylonians were one of the first people to record the zodiac, a few hundred years BC.

In ancient times, people experienced a close connection to the earth and the celestial realm. The adage 'As above, so below', that the movement of the planets and stars mirrored life on earth and human affairs, made perfect sense. Essentially, we were all one, and ancient people sought symbolic meaning in everything around them.

We are living in a very different world now, in

which scientific truth is paramount; yet many people are still seeking meaning. In a world where you have an abundance of choice, dominated by the social media culture that allows complete visibility into other people's lives, it can be hard to feel you belong or find purpose or think that the choices you are making are the right ones.

It's this calling for something more, the sense that there's a more profound truth beyond the objective and scientific, that leads people to astrology and similar disciplines that embrace a universal truth, an intuitive knowingness. Today astrology has a lot in common with spirituality, meditation, the Law of Attraction, a desire to know the cosmic order of things.

Astrology means 'language of the stars' and people today are rediscovering the usefulness of ancient wisdom. The universe is always talking to you; there are signs if you listen and the more you tune in, the more you feel guided by life. This is one of astrology's significant benefits, helping you to make sense of an increasingly unpredictable world.

Used well, astrology can guide you in making the best possible decisions in your life. It's an essential skill in your personal toolbox that enables you to navigate the ups and downs of life consciously and efficiently.

About this book

Astrology is an ancient art that helps you find meaning in the world. The majority of people to this day know their star sign, and horoscopes are growing increasingly popular in the media and online.

The modern reader understands that star signs are a helpful reference point in life. They not only offer valuable self-insight and guidance, but are indispensable when it comes to understanding other people, and living and working together in harmony.

This new and innovative pocket guide updates the ancient tradition of astrology to make it relevant and topical for today. It distils the wisdom of the star signs into an up-to-date format that's easy to read and digest, and fun and informative too. Covering a broad range of topics, it offers you insight and understanding into many different areas of your life. There are some unique sections you won't find anywhere else.

The style of the guide is geared towards you being able to maximise your strengths, so you can live well and use your knowledge of your star sign to your advantage. The more in tune you are with your zodiac sign, the higher your potential to lead a happy and fulfilled life.

The guide starts with a quick introduction to your star sign, in bullet point format. This not only reveals your star sign's ancient ruling principles, but brings astrology up-to-date, with your star sign mission, an appropriate quote for your sign and how best to describe your star sign in a tweet.

The first chapter is called 'Be True To Your Sign' and is one of the most important sections in the guide. It's a comprehensive look at all aspects of your star sign, helping define what makes you special, and explaining how the rich symbolism of your zodiac sign can reveal more about your character. For example, being born at a specific time of year and in a particular season is significant in itself.

This chapter focuses in depth on the individual attributes of your star sign in a way that's positive and uplifting. It offers a holistic view of your sign and is meant to inspire you. Within this section, you find out the reasons why your star sign traits and characteristics are unique to you.

There's a separate chapter towards the end of the guide that takes this star sign information to a new level. It's called 'Your Cosmic Gifts and Talents' and tells you what's individual about you from your star sign perspective. Most importantly, it highlights your skills and strengths, offering you clear examples of how to make the most of your natural birthright.

The guide touches on another important aspect of your star sign, in the chapters entitled 'Your Shadow Side' and 'Your Star Sign Secrets'. This reveals the potential weaknesses inherent within your star sign, and the tricks and habits you can fall into if you're not aware of them. The star sign secrets might surprise you.

There's guidance here about what you can focus on to minimise the shadow side of your star sign, and this is linked in particular to your opposite sign of the zodiac. You learn how opposing forces complement each other when you hold both ends of the spectrum, enabling them to work together.

Essentially, the art of astrology is about how to find balance in your life, to gain a sense of universal or cosmic order, so you feel in flow rather than pulled in different directions.

Other chapters in the guide provide revealing information about your love life and sex life. There are cosmic tips on how to work to your star sign strengths so you can attract and keep a fulfilling relationship, and lead a joyful sex life. There's also a guide to your love compatibility with all twelve star signs.

Career, money and prosperity is another essential section in the guide. These chapters offer you vital information on your purpose in life, and how to make the most of your potential out in the world. Your star sign skills and strengths are revealed, including what sort of job or profession suits you.

There are also helpful suggestions about what to avoid and what's not a good choice for you. There's a list of traditional careers associated with your star sign, to give you ideas about where you can excel in life if you require guidance on your future direction.

Also, there are chapters in the book on practical matters, like your health and well-being, your food and diet. These recommend the right kind of exercise for you, and how you can increase your vitality and nurture your mind, body and soul, depending on your star sign. There are individual yoga poses and tarot cards that have been carefully selected for you.

Further chapters reveal unique star sign information about your image and style. This includes whether there's a particular fashion that suits you, and how you can accentuate your look and make the most of your body.

There are even chapters that can help you decide where to go on holiday and who with, and how to decorate your home. There are some fun sections, including ideal gifts for your star sign, and ideas for films, books and music specific to your star sign.

Also, the guide has a comprehensive birthday section so you can find out which famous people share your birthday. You can discover who else is born under your star sign, people who may be your role models and whose careers or gifts you can aspire to. There are celebrity examples throughout the guide too, revealing more about the unique characteristics of your star sign.

At the end of the guide, there's a Question and Answer section, which explains the astrological terms used in the guide. It also offers answers to some general questions that often arise around astrology.

This theme is continued in a useful section entitled Additional Information. This describes the symmetry of astrology and shows you how different patterns connect the twelve star signs. If you're a beginner to astrology, this is your next stage, learning about the elements, the modes and the houses.

View this book as your blueprint, your guide to you and your future destiny. Enjoy discovering astrological revelations about you, and use this pocket guide to learn how to live well and find happiness according to your star sign.

A QUICK GUIDE TO LIBRA

• • • • •

Libra Birthdays: 23 September to 23 October

Zodiac Symbol: The Scales

Ruling Planet: Venus

Mode/Element: Cardinal Air

Colour: Pink, pastel colours

Part of the Body: Kidneys and lower back

Day of the Week: Friday

Top Traits: Diplomatic, Charming, Peace-loving

Your Star Sign Mission: to honour love, to inspire cooperation and reconciliation

Best At: mediating, discriminating, considering both sides of the coin, negotiating, analysing, people skills and relating, sharing, buying gifts, bringing people together, social etiquette

Weaknesses: indecisive, pleasing, can't say 'no', lazy, wishy-washy

Key Phrase: I relate

Libra Quote: 'If music be the food of love, play on.' Duke Orsino, *Twelfth Night*

How to describe Libra in a Tweet: Romantic, clever, loves culture & art. Discerning, a good judge. Tendency to be lazy & indecisive. Fave question: 'What do you think?'

● ● ● ● ●

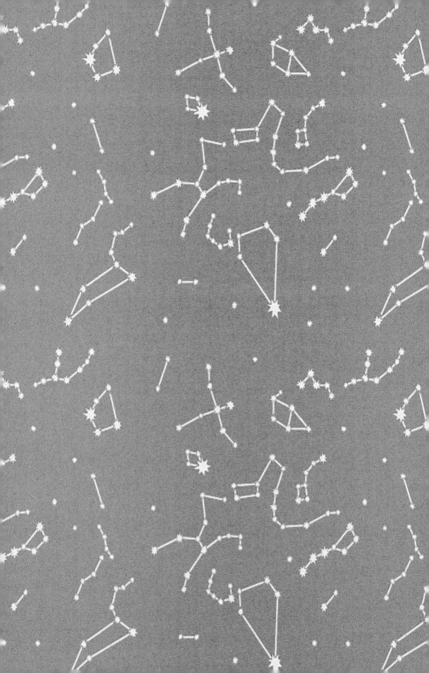

Be True To Your Sign

• • • • •

Ruled by seductive Venus, you are the love god/goddess of the zodiac. You are happiest when you are engaged in all things lovely, where you can sing and dance your way through life, preferably with a partner on your arm. Intelligent, cultured and interested in the arts as you are, your Libra vote is for equality, and in any dispute or negotiation you aim for a fair outcome.

When the Sun enters your sign it heralds the Equinox, the start of autumn in the northern hemisphere and the start of spring in the southern hemisphere. Therefore, Libra is one of four key markers in the astrological year; the two Equinoxes and the two Solstice points, which define the changes of season.

In astrology, this marks the start of a new chapter and Libra is one of the four cardinal signs – the others being Aries, Cancer and Capricorn – which hold an important role in the star sign pantheon. You are the bearer of a new beginning, and the cardinal signs are the leaders of the zodiac, paving the way for a fresh start.

The Equinox is a time when day and night, or light and dark, are in equal balance. This is fitting for Libra, whose zodiac symbol is the Scales. Your sign, more than any other, is about finding balance in life and you are often preoccupied realigning the scales of your own life and the lives of others.

Ultimately, as a Sun Libra, you seek harmony, balance and a sense of peace. The irony, however, is that when you find happiness/equilibrium/an ideal way of life, it rarely remains static for long. Instead, the scales are constantly recalibrating and begin to shift almost immediately once they are steady. Getting the balance of life 'just right' can be a never-ending Libra activity.

But don't let this stop you, because this is where your sign excels. This is your cosmic masterpiece. You have the ability to hold the opposite ends of an axis, to consider both sides of the equation, to be involved in negotiation, to look at how there can be a fair solution for one and all.

Your zodiac symbol, the Scales, is representative of the scales of justice and often you will see Libra represented by a hand holding a scales. It is significant that you are one of the zodiac signs represented not by an animal but by a human being. These signs, the others being Gemini, Virgo and Aquarius, are called humane signs and they are courteous and involved in human interactions.

This is significant for you because your element is air, which represents mental agility. Air signs are sociable. They get involved in the networks of life and communication is paramount. This gives you the ability to detach from your emotions, and offer a fair and impartial response. You are brilliant at analysing, evaluating and creating a working plan.

17

If you're a typical Libra, you have a lively mind and you're naturally bright and articulate. You're a strategist at heart and the world of ideas is a constant fascination for you. You always want to hear both sides of the story, to know what everyone's thinking, to be fully informed. Only then do you try to find a resolution or make sense of what you've learned.

This side of your character, however, can create a challenge and in your own life, you may find it almost impossible to make decisions. You regularly weigh up all the options and you can see so many different alternatives that you talk yourself in and out of them and go round in circles.

This process gets even more complicated if you then ask other people what they think you should do and end up with all their suggestions as well. Learning how to discern the best possible course of action is something that can take you time and possibly drive you mad in the process.

One of the skills you need to learn in your lifetime is to hold fast, to take up your position and remain rooted. It can take the classic Libra a while to discover how to put self first, others second.

As a Libra, you are the people person extraordinaire of the zodiac and a Libra who's alone or without other people to keep them company can quickly fade. You need people in your life to bounce ideas off, to share experiences with and to enhance your enjoyment of life.

This makes sense when you know that Libra rules the seventh house of the zodiac, the part of the horoscope connected to people, partnership, the 'other'. This is where you learn more about yourself: through your relationships, both personal and professional. Human interaction is your lifeblood, it's how you breathe and what restores you and nurtures you.

Your ruling planet Venus is linked to relationships and in particular romantic love, and if you are true to your sign of Libra, you are one of life's romantics. Whether you're married, divorced, falling in love or breaking up, relationships are your Number One priority. It is the major theme that runs through your life.

The classic Libra continually creates partnerships in their life, both romantic and otherwise. People matter to you, and not only in your own life but in the world in general. Yours is the sign most closely linked to peace and a definitive Libra motto would be 'Make love, not war'. You are not confrontational by nature and if anything, you prefer to steer clear of arguments or fall-outs.

Eastern philosophy with its focus on unity and oneness appeals to your Libra nature. A typical Libra gains much from beliefs that encompass peace and enlightenment, and you often play an active role in political causes and spiritual movements. This is Libra's domain.

Venus, your ruling planet, is not only the goddess

of love but is also linked to art and beauty. You revere beauty in whichever shape or form, and admire feminine qualities. You have a discerning eye for beauty in all its guises and the quintessential Libra helps to make the world a better or a more beautiful place.

The main conundrum for your sign, however, is that you are constantly changing as your Libra scales dip and realign. You can be extraordinarily proactive for a while and then collapse and do nothing, hence your zodiac nickname 'lazy Libra'. First you overindulge in the pursuit of pleasure and then you're suddenly virtuous and pure – or holier-than-thou.

In general, however, the Libra nature is all about love, beauty, sweetness and harmony. You know that sometimes all it takes is for you to switch on your Libra dimple and charm your way through life with your gorgeous smile.

Your Shadow Side

You are renowned as the most charming sign of the zodiac and it's true that the quintessential Libra has core skills of persuasion, negotiation and diplomacy. You know how to win other people over to your way of thinking and a full-on Libra charm offensive can lead to spectacular results.

However, there is another side of the Libra nature that can kick in and push your ability to persuade to the extreme. Then you become scheming, calculating, manipulative or even controlling to get your way.

This is a classic Libra puzzle that can cause an ongoing internal struggle. How do you hold firm to the Libra values of harmony and fairness, initiating and making a stand for all that you believe in or for what you want, without being confrontational? Of course, there will be times in your life when you come up against opposition, that's the way of the world.

What can be confusing for other people, however, is that you rarely go about things in a way that's direct or honest, because inside you're conflicted. You want to come across as fair and non-intimidating but this isn't always possible. Trying to keep everyone happy, and trying to assert your own needs without other people taking offence or opposing you, is rarely simple.

You don't want to look shallow or weak either and yet if you invariably take the middle ground or change your mind regularly, this not only creates inner conflict but also leaves other people feeling perplexed. You end up saying one thing but meaning another and the end result is insincerity, the very quality you wish to avoid.

This is what your sign of Libra needs to learn in life: how to stand true for what you believe in and who you are without allowing your inner ambivalence to prevail.

This is where you can learn a lot from your opposite sign of Aries. All signs of the zodiac take on certain characteristics from their opposite sign. As a Libra, you have to develop the ability to be direct, which is Aries strength. You may find this difficult to do, but it will make your beloved relationships easier to handle and you'll feel more fulfilled in your personal agenda.

One of the biggest Libra challenges is learning to say No. People-pleasing might give the right impression, but ultimately it doesn't do a lot for your self-esteem or for gaining genuine respect from others.

Until you learn the lessons of your shadow side, you spend a lot of time complaining that 'It's not fair'. Once you recognise that it's up to you to take responsibility for your actions and not to worry overly about what other people think, then life, in general, becomes a whole lot easier.

Your Star Sign Secrets

Shhh, don't tell anyone but your greatest fear is FOMO – the fear of missing out. You are the social Queen Bee of the zodiac and you want to know what's going on in everyone's lives: your friends, your partner, your family, your colleagues, your children. It can cause you endless head-aches hearing what other people are up to when you've not been invited. This is Libra's star sign secret.

You have another secret too and this relates to the lazy side of your character that loves to lounge around and be indulgent. If you're a typical Libra, there's a part of your nature that would be quite happy in life doing nothing and letting other people do all the work or look after you.

It's not really the image you want to portray to the world. You know you have a lot to give and yet there's a part of you that would be quite happy if other people waited on you.

Your Love Life

Knowing about your star sign is an absolute essential when it comes to love and relationships. Once you understand what drives you, nurtures you and keeps you happy in love, then you can be true to who you are rather than try to be someone you're not.

Plus, once you recognise your weak points when it comes to relationships (and everyone has them), you can learn to moderate them and focus instead on boosting your strengths to find happiness in love.

> **KEY CONCEPTS:** romantic fairy tale, serial monogamist, over-giving, love triangles, forgiveness and tolerance

Cosmic Tip: Work out whether you're more yin or yang. Then find your counterpart for a perfectly balanced relationship.

As a Libra, you are one of life's romantics and if you're true to your sign you wear your heart on your sleeve. You can charm the birds from the trees and it doesn't take you long to become an expert in the art of romance. Lovely Libra loves nothing more than falling in love.

In fact, relationships can become your life's mission. Whether you're in love, out of love or somewhere in-between, love is a constant source of interest and delight. You, more than any other star sign, are likely to believe in true love and the idea that Mr/Ms Right is out there somewhere.

Plus, you're someone who enjoys all that romance has to offer. You expect a potential partner to be attentive and make an effort, and it boosts a person's attractiveness levels when they take charge and go out of their way to arrange a special or romantic occasion.

Libra women in particular often have fantasies of a big white wedding and an idyllic family life. You want the romantic fairy tale with all the trimmings. Sometimes, however, you have to be careful that you don't leap in too fast and have a ring on your partner's finger before you've got to know each other well.

That said, marriage proposals, weddings and anniversaries are incredibly important to you as a Libra, because they give you some of your happiest memories in life. And woe betide your partner if they forget your special day.

Many a Sun Libra will experience a happy love life and if you find someone you're compatible with, you throw yourself heart and soul into the relationship. There's a side to your nature that's attracted to people who are different from you, whether by age, culture or background. You love bringing opposites together and finding out how you can complement each other.

It is important that any relationship you're in is based on equality. There might be a part of you that's happy to let your other half make all the decisions or primarily look after you, but ultimately it won't lead to fulfilment.

You need to find your own sense of self within a love relationship, rather than give yourself over completely to another person. In a similar vein, it's important that you learn who you are separate from your role within a relationship, and every Libra can benefit from spending some time alone at some point in their lives.

Having the Sun in Libra, a place where it's not traditionally strong, can mean you try to fit in and become who someone else wants you to be. A good relationship will act as a mirror in that it reveals who you are more than compensating for who you're not.

Alternatively, you might be the type of Libra who is so in love with romance that you become a serial monogamist or find pleasure through your romantic conquests. Libra men tend to have this propensity more and if you're a typical 'Don Juan' Libra, your capacity for seduction knows no bounds. It's true too that many Libra men are happiest in the company of women.

Male or female, as a Libra you can work your charm on whoever you please and this can give you a reputation for being flirtatious or even sleazy. Also, you sometimes get caught up in love triangles. You're fair but not always faithful and this usually comes about because you hate to disappoint anyone and you can't say no.

In love, whether you're an eager-to-please Libra or you're the one who's leading the way, it is vital in your relationship to ensure that both partners' needs are met. This is where happiness can be found.

Sometimes you need to learn to speak up for what you want and not let another person get away with behaviour that doesn't work for you. This is where the non-confrontational side of your character that tends towards avoidance can leave you at a disadvantage in a love relationship.

You don't like major outbursts if you're a typical Libra and an overly emotional partner will test you. Arguing can be healthy, however, as this is a way for both of you to find out what the other person wants and get your needs met.

You tend to see the best in people but this is where it's extra important that you learn to trust your instincts. Question your partner's behaviour when it's suspicious, even if it means provoking a row.

35

The Libra law is that a relationship based on compromise and equality is more likely to satisfy both of you. Just don't fall into the Libra trap of being so easy-going and laid-back that another person can easily take advantage of you.

When you're happy in love, you want to ensure that your other half is happy too and this is where you're a delight to be around. You can be silly and loving in equal measure and you love nothing more than going all out to ensure your life together is warm, connected and bags of fun.

Even when a love relationship ends, it's unlikely that you'll waste much time hating the other person. In fact, a typical Libra often remains friends with ex-lovers. A classic Libra response to a break-up is to recognise that you shared a lot in common and stay on good terms.

It's no surprise that the recent trend of 'conscious uncoupling' was instigated by a Sun Libra, Gwyneth Paltrow (28 September). Love is love and this is what your sign of Libra knows inherently. In love relationships, your default mode of behaviour is kind, forgiving and tolerant.

Your Love Matches

Some star signs are a better love match for you than others. The classic combinations are the other two star signs from the same element as your sign, air; in Libra's case, Gemini and Aquarius.

In any relationship, you tend to focus on the positives of the other person rather than the negatives, certainly in the beginning. Your interactions with other people are one of your greatest joys and you won't leave any star sign stone unturned in your pursuit of love perfection.

You know instinctively that any star sign match can be a good match as long as you're both willing to learn from each other and use astrological insight to find out more about what makes the other person tick. Here's a quick guide to your love matches with all twelve star signs.

Libra–Aries: Opposites Attract

You tend to avoid conflict and you always consider the other person's opinion or point of view, whereas Aries is naturally assertive and decisive. Libra rules fairness and justice and Aries rules passion and anger. Together you teach each other about compromise and how to get needs met.

Libra–Taurus: Soulmates

Libra and Taurus are the two signs of the zodiac ruled by romantic Venus. This is a warm and tender combination. Both of you have an innate understanding of the importance of beauty in the world and in your immediate surroundings.

Libra–Gemini: In Your Element

This is one of the chattiest combinations in the zodiac as you are both naturally sociable. Your sign loves to be in love and Gemini can flirt, so trust plays a big part in the success of this relationship. You share a love of sightseeing, people-watching and cultural events.

Libra–Cancer: Squaring Up To Each Other

Your relationship has a feminine vibe. You both ease into attachment relationships and enjoy having loved ones with whom you can share everything. As long as Cancer appreciates your need for intimacy and detachment, it's a comfortable and caring combination.

Libra–Leo: Sexy Sextiles

Both of you understand the importance of paying attention to your partner's needs. Anniversaries and romantic dates are significant and woe betide if either of you forget to mark those important occasions. This combination requires a high romance factor at all times.

Libra–Virgo: Next-Door Neighbours

A refined and cultured match, this is a romantic pairing. Both you and Virgo appreciate beauty and order and you enjoy sampling the finer things in life. A meeting of minds and a healthy work/life balance are on the cards when you learn to appreciate each other fully.

Libra–Libra: Two Peas In A Pod

Libra and Libra fit together hand in glove and you can be delightful as one half of a match made in heaven. A loving relationship is your ideal scenario in life, your fairy-tale dream come true. Enjoying a shared social life keeps your relationship lively and fresh.

Libra–Scorpio: Next-Door Neighbours

Ruled by Venus and Mars respectively, Libra and Scorpio are the cosmic lovers of the zodiac. A tempestuous but loving match, this love affair can reach mythic proportions. Issues may arise if you try to keep love light when Scorpio wants to go in deep and demands loyalty.

Libra–Sagittarius: Sexy Sextiles

The two of you have to develop trust and loyalty. You share a love of the good things in life and as long as your relationship is chock-full of stimulating experiences, love can thrive. Participating in an activity or hobby together keeps you interested in each other.

Libra–Capricorn: Squaring Up To Each Other

This is a stylish combination and the two of you share a love of good taste, decorum and social niceties. You have a discerning and artistic eye; Capricorn has a dignified and respectful manner. A match to admire, but it's what lies underneath that determines whether your loving bond is real.

Libra–Aquarius: In Your Element

This combination pits the romantic (Libra) with the individual (Aquarius). You two keep the relationship alive when you deepen your love within the realm of the weird or unconventional. You may dream of a perfect white wedding but Aquarius is a hippy at heart.

Libra–Pisces: Soulmates

Libra and Pisces are ruled by Venus and Neptune respectively. Neptune is said to be the higher octave of Venus and this is a poetic, artistic and

43

sensitive combination. An intuitive and romantic match that can create magic when you discover your soul connection.

Your Sex Life

. . . . .

If lovemaking were an art, your paintbrush would create a masterpiece every time. If it was down to you, you would devote much of your energy to the practice of love and the art of lovemaking.

When it comes to wooing your partner, no one else comes close to doing it better. You are a true romantic and love poems, romantic movies and true-life love stories can all help to get you in the mood for love.

Champagne breakfasts and romantic weekends are also high on your list of mood-enhancing activities. Being such a lover of romance, sometimes you enjoy the build-up to sex the most.

Certainly, it's an integral part of the whole package as far as you're concerned.

Satin sheets and champagne in bed are one way to turn you on. And there must be plenty of kissing and sensual exploration of each other's bodies before you're ready to indulge in the sexual act.

Sex isn't just a physical act for you; there needs to be a mental connection too, in line with your air sign character. You need to know that the other person likes you for who you are in addition to finding you attractive.

Sex in a romantic setting is a great turn-on, as is something slightly saucy, e.g. going out to dinner at an exclusive restaurant, only to reveal to your lover that you're wearing no underwear.

Your ruler Venus represents feminine qualities but in our modern world, we have lost some of what Venus represents and what being a woman means.

For example, in Roman mythology, Venus was the goddess of prostitutes, although she could turn the hearts of men and women from sexual vice to virtue. In other words, Venus ruled all aspects of love (think of the term venereal disease, which derives from the word Venus).

So explore all that love and sex has to offer. Libra Dakota Johnson (4 October) was the perfect actor to take on the female lead role in the film adaptation of the erotic, romantic book *Fifty Shades of Grey* (2015).

If you want some extra titillation to get you and your lover ready for action, then head for a burlesque show. Burlesque has developed over time from the bawdy and scandalous to the art form it is today. One of the top exponents of burlesque, who helped to popularise its revival, is Dita von Teese (28 September).

A true Libra adores beauty and you love all the parts of sex that are beautiful or romantic. If they aren't, you'd rather not do them; it spoils the mood. You are one of the signs of the zodiac who may find oral sex distasteful, for example. Or at least, you prefer it with some degree of cleanliness and lots of sweet-smelling perfumes wafting around the room.

You want to be able to look into your partner's eyes during lovemaking and your need for equality spreads to the bedroom too. A sexual position where you both get to share the work – and the pleasure – is ideal for your sign; give and take. You want lovemaking to be a romantic act and if you can both say 'I love you' and mean it afterwards, that's the Libra ideal.

If you're going through a single phase in your life, this gives you time and space to work out what you want from a relationship and to line up some new fantasies for next time.

LIBRA ON A FIRST DATE

- You spend ages getting ready and choosing what to wear

- You notice immediately whether or not your date has made an effort

- You're impressed by good manners and hate vulgarity

- You want to ensure the other person has a good time

- You end up talking about your past relationships

Your Friends and Family

You are one of the sociable air signs and your sign is linked to relating. Put the two together and friends are incredibly important in your life. In fact, it's rare that a Libra doesn't have a wide circle of friends and a busy social network.

The definitive Libra loves parties, group events and girls' or boys' nights in or out. A chance to dress up and hang out at a glamorous location and meet new people is every Libra's dream. When you feel sure of yourself and you're in confident Libra mood, you love to work a room and catch up on all the gossip.

You may even be one of the enviable Libra set who find it easy to charm their way through life, winning over other people and using their connections to get invited to exclusive events. The classic Libra personality can open many a door.

You care a lot about your friends too, especially those close to your heart. You're often the first to suggest a social get-together and you like to stay involved in your buddies' lives. If you're a typical Libra, you'll shower your close friends with thoughtful gifts and you're rarely one to miss a birthday.

In fact, you often end up being the social secretary, the person in your group of friends who organises a big night out or buys everyone tickets for a show. Love is never far away from the agenda either, so knowing about your friends' love lives is a must and you excel at matchmaking. You like to see your friends happy in love and you will do all that you can to help.

Falling out with friends can be a nightmare for you and it often causes you a lot of pain if other people are mean or leave you out. This is particularly the case when growing up but it can be an issue at any age for the definitive Libra.

You are a natural at sorting out friendship disputes, although not necessarily your own. But one of the Libra skills is your ability to see the bigger picture, to be intimate yet detached and to gain an accurate perspective of any people situation.

You're rarely bitchy unless you have been hurt; instead, you're likely to see the other person's point of view in any argument or dispute. You do have to be wary of always asking other people's opinions, though, or saying 'What do you think?'

In a similar vein, you might end up apologising when you've done nothing wrong and if you're taking the blame for everything, stop and take notice. The more self-belief you have and the better you know yourself, the easier your friendships become.

Like any relationship in your life, a friendship requires give and take and that means sometimes being assertive and at other times letting the other person take the lead. Being an air sign, you can't help but play devil's advocate, especially as you always see both sides of the coin. Regularly airing your thoughts, however, isn't always the fast-track route to friendship success.

As a Libra, you do have to learn to stop worrying about what other people think. Once you get to a place in your life where you recognise your own attractiveness and you have good self-esteem, then you make life easier for yourself.

You have a natural tendency to gloss over anything ugly or cruel and even in your friendships, you're not always happy delving into difficult topics. Sometimes other people accuse you of being shallow or insincere. Usually, this stems from the fact that you like to focus on the positives in life rather than what's negative or dark.

The classic Libra is an expert at social etiquette and good manners. In friendship as in life, you expect an equal flow of talking and listening and you quickly grow bored of anyone who doesn't understand the bare essentials of a relationship.

Within your family, you often fall into the role of peacemaker. You're the one who wants everyone to get along well and you will go out of your way to ensure that harmony reigns.

Growing up in a difficult or argumentative family can be a challenge for you and often it's only when you have your own family that things start to fall into place. This is when you appreciate being around people who make the best of life rather than the opposite.

Ideally, as a parent, you want to be best friends with your child or children, especially when they're older. Discipline can be an issue for you. There's a side of your Libra nature that will happily indulge your kids, and then you flip into being overly strict, even a military type of parenting. As in all areas of Libra life, it's about finding the right balance.

Your Health and Well-Being

> **KEY CONCEPTS:** a balanced diet, sweet tooth, making exercise fun, beautiful food, all things in moderation.

The Libra lifestyle is a constant search for balance and the same principle applies to your health and well-being. To feel well, you need harmony in your surroundings and your relationships and when things are out of kilter, it can disturb your metabolism.

You don't like to confront what's difficult in your life but that means you don't always deal with things in a manner that's straightforward and efficient. You can be incredibly indecisive and you worry endlessly about upsetting others, what to say, the right thing to do.

If there's disruption at your place of work or you work in an environment that's noisy or dirty, this too can adversely affect your equilibrium. And, especially, if you're going through a troubled patch in your life, this impacts not only on your mood but your diet as well.

So ensuring you have a healthy and harmonious lifestyle is important for you. Rather than try to get too strict with yourself when it comes to exercise and diet, here too it's best to keep a healthy perspective on your capabilities.

You're not the most disciplined of the star signs and you can be easily led astray. If it's a toss-up between going to the gym or going out to lunch with a friend, the social, indulgent option is likely to win time and again.

So trick yourself into healthy living by keeping your exercise schedule fun and varied. Do a yoga class one week and then go to a Zumba class the following week. If you're a typical Libra, you will love dancing; so factor some exercise into your socialising too by signing up for a dance class with a friend, whether you love ballroom or you're more of a disco queen/king.

Any form of exercise class is going to work better for you if it's sociable and you're hanging out with people whose company you enjoy. Water sports aren't usually your thing, which makes sense being an air sign. Walking in the fresh air is an excellent way to be in your element – literally – and get fit at the same time.

Positive affirmations can work well for you and it's a good idea to have a few morale-boosting quotes where you can see them as you go about your daily routine – fridge magnets, a book open by your bedside or on your desk where you work. Happiness comes from the inside and little reminders go a long way towards lifting your spirits.

For you it's not about being at peak physical fitness, but more about feeling well and happy in your mind, body and soul. As a Libra toxic relationships impact detrimentally on you, so take this into account. As much as possible, make sure you're around people who are positive rather than individuals who are negative.

Your ruler Venus is linked to the five senses; sight, taste, smell, touch and hearing. Therefore, anything you can do on a daily level that soothes or uplifts your senses is worth pursuing. Libra rules sweet-smelling flowers, such as roses, lilies and jasmine.

Treating yourself to flowers every now and again ticks off two senses at once: sight and smell. Or grow pots of scented flowers outside your door so you get a gentle waft of their perfume on your way out. Aromatherapy oils are also a great way to give your spirits a quick boost.

More than anything, however, make sure you find time to relax on a regular basis, to indulge the side of your nature that enjoys being idle and comfortable. Be more Zen, zone out with ambient music and find your own little place of Libra calm.

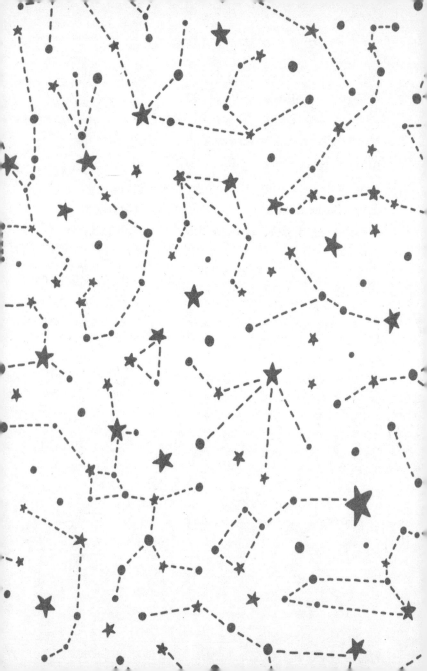

Libra and Food

The part of the body associated with Libra is the kidneys. If they're functioning well, you have two of them, creating a perfect symmetry, and their function is cleansing. The kidneys keep the blood in the body balanced to maintain good health. Therefore a balanced diet works best for you and too much excess of either food or alcohol can leave you feeling ill.

Also, Venus is your ruling planet and Venusian

delights in all guises are Libra's indulgence. Venus rules the sweet things in life, including food and drink, and if you're a typical Libra, you will have a sweet tooth and a penchant for sugar.

Present a Libra with some colourful macaroons, pastel-coloured cupcakes or chocolate truffles and the response is rarely negative. You're a soft touch for pretty food, and it's not only about the taste for you but how good the confectionery looks and smells.

Afternoon tea, a French patisserie, a traditional sweet shop: as a Libra, you probably have your favourite. And a meal without dessert is rarely your idea of the perfect dining experience.

If you're a typical Libra, you do have to watch how much you eat and if you have a sweet tooth, try to choose small bites over large portions. Or steer yourself towards the fruit bowl, as fruit including apples, pears, cherries, peaches and, in particular, soft fruit like strawberries, is ruled by your planet Venus.

Japanese food, nouvelle cuisine and edible flowers all have their place on the Libra table. Your ideal food is beautiful to look at as well as delectable to the palate – food as art. Opt for delicate and sweet flavours and herbs ruled by Venus, such as mint, thyme and sorrel.

If you're very health-conscious, clean eating often appeals to you, or cleansing your body by eliminating certain foods. Drinking plenty of water helps to flush out the kidneys too.

And it's not uncommon for your sign to channel your peace-loving beliefs into the animal world and become vegan or vegetarian. One of the greatest advocates for vegetarian food has been Libra Linda McCartney (24 September).

Ultimately, however, for Libra it's all about balance and recognising that when your emotions are off balance, you're more likely to comfort-eat. Love yourself, love your diet.

Do You Look Like A Libra?

Libra is known as one of the best-looking signs of the zodiac. Your ruler Venus is female and both Libra men and women are often easy on the eye.

This isn't to say that you're someone who flaunts your looks; this kind of Libra is rare. Instead, you tend to be blissfully unaware of how good-looking you are and you're the opposite of a show-off.

You know instinctively how to accentuate your good features and tone down the parts of your body that you're not as comfortable with. You are often softly-spoken too, rather than loud and brash.

Libra is associated with classic beauty and is the sign of symmetry. Look for regular features, a sensual mouth, almond-shaped eyes and the Libra giveaway, a dimple in the chin or on the cheek.

In the Libra woman, the hair tends to be flowing and light; and both Libra men and women like to style their hair. You walk with grace and poise and good deportment comes naturally to you. It's your smile that radiates the most, however, as you're usually genuinely pleased to be in other people's company.

Your Style and Image

When it comes to style, Libra leads the way. You have a natural elegance and grace and you can pull off any outfit and still look a million dollars.

A classic Libra will be a follower of fashion, whether male or female, and looking good makes you feel good. You can throw on clothes without much thought and attention and look stunning. If you're a typical Libra, however, you're likely to put a lot of thought into what you wear. You want to look coordinated and you know instinctively which items in your wardrobe work well together.

Light and bright colours suit you best, and clothes that move with a natural flow. Two iconic Libra designers are Ralph Lauren (14 October) and Donna Karan (2 October) and their style of clothes suit your sign: sleek lines, simple cuts and classic tailoring.

For a big night out, the Libra woman wants to tap into her inner goddess and you can look fantastic in a fitting dress that shows off your curves. Pastel colours and small additions such as a carefully placed bow or pretty belt add to the feminine look.

If you're a classic Libra, you'll always look stylish, but at the same time you like to fit in rather than stand out. Turning up in the 'wrong' dress code can be a Libra nightmare.

Grooming is essential to the Libra character and Libra women tend to spend more on make-up and beauty treatments than the average person. Libra men too like to take care of their looks and quality skincare and even subtle make-up isn't out of the question. A powerfully scented aftershave or perfume is an essential part of the Libra toilette.

Some people might think you're vain but taking care of your appearance is an integral part of who you are. In fact, you're one of the signs of the zodiac more likely to invest in cosmetic surgery.

When it comes to buying clothes, you head for the designer rather than the cheap rails as you prefer quality items. That's not to say you aren't a natural at cheap chic and if anyone can find a perfect outfit in a charity shop, it's your sign. Heels too look good on you and that includes the men.

Your Home

Your Ideal Libra Home:

Your dream home would be graceful and elegant, a shrine to modern art and beautiful objects, situated on a hill with magnificent panoramic views. You and your friends would be waited on by staff so you could relax in style in the lap of luxury.

Your planet Venus rules beauty and harmony, which is why your home must be attractive to the eye. If you are a typical Libra, beautiful places are a tonic for you and your home will reflect this.

Yours is the sign most closely linked with style and you have a natural flair and an instinctive eye for what looks good. You appreciate symmetry in design, in line with your zodiac symbol, the Scales.

That's not to say that the look of every room has to be precise, but often where there's an empty space, you will balance it out with a perfectly chosen lamp or plant. The definitive Libra would naturally choose a pair of ornaments to complete the symmetrical effect.

You enjoy a sense of movement, space and fluidity in your home and your style includes drapes and soft furnishings. Gentle curves are easy on the eye and your home must be a place of comfort.

The colours associated with Libra are the pastel colours – pale blue, mint green, peach, but especially pink, traditionally lighter shades of pink rather than vibrant neon pink.

Your style is feminine rather than frilly. However, you are attracted to anything pretty and you appreciate beautiful ornaments and objects around the home. Coloured glass, attractive candles, stylish lamps; you like your home to be filled with carefully chosen pieces that give you pleasure.

Social occasions were made for you and your home must be the ideal place to entertain. You adore cocktail parties and you prefer to serve canapés or a light buffet rather than food that's too heavy.

One of the countries linked with Libra is Japan, and the peaceful style of the Zen culture suits your need for a quiet space in which to relax. You love to listen to different music depending on your mood, and you may have wind chimes or Tibetan bells somewhere in your home. You probably play a musical instrument and if anyone loves dancing, it's you. Space to whirl around at home, even in the kitchen, is an immediate mood-lifter.

You don't usually like to live on your own and as your sign is associated with relating, you enjoy having a partner in your life. Matching sets can appeal, whether it's 'his and hers' bathrobes, kitchen sets or coordinated towels.

You are a romantic at heart and you don't like being around anything that's offensive to the senses. Your bedroom is often a serene haven and you're more likely to choose a four-poster bed with white cotton sheets and muslin curtains than anything overtly sexy.

You hate to feel rushed and at the end of the day, you prefer to relax in comfort. Either slipping into your PJs as soon as you get home from work or having beautiful and cosy cashmere throws to snuggle under as you watch a DVD is your idea of home heaven.

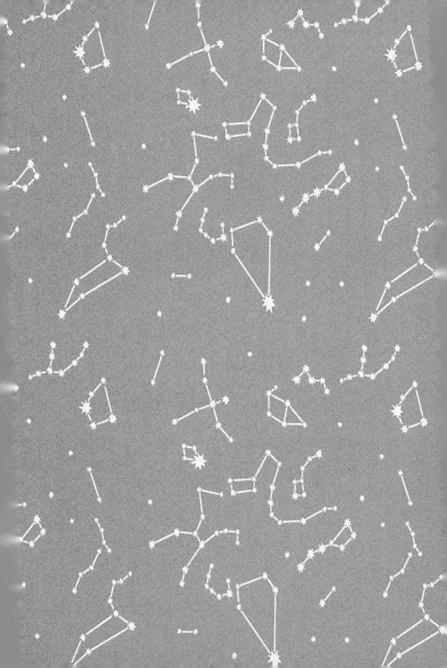

Your Star Sign Destinations

IDEAS FOR LIBRA:

- *a tour of Europe to visit the top art galleries*

- *a pampering break at a spa hotel*

- *a holiday to Japan – for the culture and cuisine*

Did you know that many cities and countries are ruled by a particular star sign? This is based on when a country was founded, although, depending on their history, sometimes places have more than one star sign attributed to them.

This can help you decide where to go on holiday and it can also be why there are certain places where you feel at home straight away.

You are one of the air signs and getting out into the fresh air, especially high up in the hills, does wonders for you. A beautiful setting, rolling hills and lots of green, Venus' colour, is good for your soul.

If you're a typical Libra, you appreciate style and culture, beauty and art. You have an eye for stunning architecture and would be equally happy exploring a European capital or one of North America's iconic cities. Immerse yourself in some of the world's top art galleries or go on a city tour so you get up close and personal with beautiful buildings, statues and palaces.

You love learning about history too, especially when you can relate it to stories of the people who lived back in the day. Exploring hand in hand with a loved one, wandering somewhere new together and stopping off at a local wine bar or restaurant is your idea of holiday heaven.

If you're true to your sign, you'll love holidaying with a group of friends. A chance to dress up and dine out in glamorous locations, people-watching and flirting with the locals, brings out the best in you.

You're not always the ideal backpacker as you tend to prefer comfort in your surroundings. Being in overly smelly or dirty surroundings is a no-no as far as you're concerned.

It's a similar story for you when it comes to summer festivals, unless the company and music more than make up for the discomfort. A chance to wear flowers in your hair and pretty festival dresses (for the Libra girls!) can be lots of fun.

Countries ruled by Libra include Burma, Tibet, Canada, Argentina, Austria, Japan

Cities ruled by Libra include Nottingham in the UK; Vienna in Austria; Lisbon in Portugal; Copenhagen in Denmark; Antwerp in Belgium; Johannesburg in South Africa

Your Career and Vocation

KEY CONCEPTS: people skills, harmonious surroundings, beauty and elegance, a clear strategy, collaborative partnerships

You might have earned the nickname 'lazy Libra' but the archetypal Libra is rarely idle. Instead, you're happiest when you find your niche in life, whether your goal is to make the world a more beautiful place or a better place.

You relate well to other people and whatever your chosen profession, you find it hard to function if you don't have anyone to bounce ideas off. You are a natural in working partnerships and a popular member of any team.

Your strengths are networking and making connections. Plus you tend to be an excellent judge of character. If you're involved in hiring and firing, you'll find the former easier than the latter.

It is important that you have a harmonious environment to work in. You will quickly become flustered, unsettled and distracted if your fellow workers are argumentative as you're likely to spend more time sorting out disputes than concentrating on your job.

You thrive when you turn your hand to different roles and, usually, you like the idea of having a varied portfolio or several jobs. Doing the same work day in, day out quickly loses its appeal.

Being self-employed only suits you if you're not working on your own. If you do run your own business, then ensure that you team up with other people on a regular basis. This might mean collaborating with other individuals who work for themselves or arranging to meet friends or contacts for coffee or lunch. Socialising is crucial for the classic Libra, both in and out of work.

Your people skills are your speciality and you flourish in an industry where making connections and bringing people together makes a difference. You have a unique ability to listen well, ask the right questions, hear different opinions, find out what people want and need and find the best solution for all concerned.

This makes you a natural in the world of mediation and you're the diplomat of the zodiac. As an air sign, you can be non-emotional too if a fair decision must be reached. This makes you an excellent judge in disputes and you excel in any career that involves sorting out people's differences or arguments. You're a natural critic as well as a mentor.

It's worth bearing in mind however that you're not someone who finds it easy to make a snap decision. In fact, you're best to avoid any work environment that's overly stressful or fast-paced. You don't like being rushed but you do have a canny knack of staying calm even under pressure.

What you are good at is analysis and evaluation and you have excellent reasoning skills. Your ability to remain impartial and to be tactful and fair can be useful in many different roles in society.

Wanting to make the world a better place is often the impetus that sees you venture into politics or a career where you can make a difference. You care deeply about other people and this can filter out into the world and give you the ambition to fight for social justice, truth and equality.

Fighting for a more peaceful world may be an

oxymoron but it's something that can be important to you. You might be the type of Libra who's tougher than you look or someone who governs with 'an iron fist in a velvet glove'.

Both UK female Prime Ministers, Margaret Thatcher (13 October) and Theresa May (1 October), were born under the sign of Libra, and you can be very successful when you step into a position of leadership.

The classic Libra archetype, however, wants to believe that peace is possible in the world without war or conflict. The most famous Libra example of a non-violent leader was Mahatma Gandhi (2 October), who inspired movements for civil rights and freedom across the world.

Another classic example is Amma (27 September), the hugging saint, whose name means Mother. Thousands of people around the world have queued up to experience a special hug from this incredible Libra lady.

Making the world a more beautiful place is another strong motivator for you and in fact, many Sun Libras are involved in industries based on beauty or creating beauty in some shape or form. You have a strong aesthetic sense and a natural aptitude for design.

You work best when your surroundings are harmonious to the senses, and you are often the team player who brings in sweet-smelling flowers or puts on music that's gentle on the ear. You like to indulge your fellow employees with little treats, especially of the confectionery kind.

There are some no-nos when it comes to your ideal working scenario and one is admin. You're not a natural dogsbody, and preferably you would employ someone else to do the painstaking work and pay attention to the details. Concentration isn't your forte and if a work task is boring, you can quickly lose interest.

Any job that's dirty or uncomfortable is worth

avoiding too. Your surroundings have a big impact on your well-being, so aim for less stress and unpleasantness and more conviviality and beauty in your life on a daily basis. This is what makes for a very happy and fulfilled Libra.

If you're seeking inspiration for a new job, take a look at the list below, which reveals the traditional careers that come under the Libra archetype:

TRADITIONAL LIBRA CAREERS

architect
stylist
hairdresser
diplomat
mediator
wedding planner
florist
fashion designer
PR executive
host/hostess
dancer/choreographer

jazz musician

politician

judge

life coach

relationship counsellor

peace ambassador

art gallery employee

chocolatier

perfumer

Your Money and Prosperity

> **KEY CONCEPTS:** a luxury lifestyle, beautiful objects, define your self-worth, laissez-faire attitude around money, bartering

One of the many attributes that your ruling planet Venus lends you is a love of all things beautiful. In general, beautiful objects, clothes, gifts and indulgences all cost money. So if you recognise that you're the type of Libra who wants to lead a luxury lifestyle, money will play an influential role in your life.

You might be lucky enough to be born into money but, if not, you need to find a way to earn enough money to maintain your chosen lifestyle. You like the finer things in life and being one of the cardinal signs, you have the potential of being a high earner because you have energy and ambition and you're good at taking the initiative.

You have a knack for using money well to make money and you're the zodiac's natural strategist. So recognise your skills and put them to good use. Whether you choose to set up a business with a partner, create a balanced finance portfolio or you charm your way to the top, do what you do best and, hopefully, the money will follow.

You're not always, however, that careful with money. Your laissez-faire attitude to life does sometimes mean you casually leave money lying around or you leave it up to someone else, your partner perhaps, to take charge of finances. Neither approach serves you well in the long run and you have to learn not to be too frivolous or flippant with money if you're to do well.

Another Libra lesson is to learn to value yourself. Once you have a strong sense of your self-worth, this will make a big difference to your wealth and prosperity. Then you can ensure that you're paid what you're worth and you can start to attract what you believe you deserve. Claim your universal right to personal entitlement.

The bartering system was made for your sign, trading skills and exchanging services. You have a natural sense of what makes a fair trade, and this can play a vital role within a community. Bringing people together to make life easier for everyone and share resources is a natural extension of your Libra skills and talents.

Your Cosmic Gifts and Talents

Double Acts

You were born to be one half of a double act. Partnerships are where you excel in life and it comes naturally for you to say 'we' rather than 'I'. You bring out the best in people and being one half of a couple brings out the best in you. So couple up, because together you're better, two's company, like attracts like.

Some of the most famous double acts include a famous Libra, e.g. Simon and Garfunkel (Paul Simon – 13 October), Ant and Dec (Declan Donnelly – 25 September), Torvill and Dean (Jayne Torvill – 7 October), French and Saunders (Dawn French – 11 October).

Be A Love Story

The world needs love and everyone enjoys a good love story, so be a love ambassador. Being a Libra, you believe in 'happy ever after' love stories; and you like to believe that love lasts even after people go their separate ways or death or tragedy intervene. You remind the rest of humanity that love knows no bounds.

Libra actress Kate Winslet (5 October) played Rose (a Libra name) in the epic film *Titanic*. She and her partner in the film, Scorpio Leonardo diCaprio, were named one of the most romantic movie couples of all time. Leonardo's

Moon in Libra matches Kate's Sun in Libra and they have what's called in astrology a 'cosmic marriage'.

Catherine Zeta-Jones (25 September) and her husband, Michael Douglas (25 September) are a classic example of a real-life Hollywood love story that's lasted many years. Born twenty-five years apart, in an example of perfect Libra harmony, they share the same birthday.

Bring People Together

You are brilliant at mediation and negotiation and it's important that you use these Libra skills somewhere in your life. You fit naturally into any relationship as the third point of the triangle and your ability to be discerning and fair can help solve many a tricky situation. Whether you're a matchmaker, a diplomat, a best friend or a peace-maker, use your natural talent to bring people together and aim for reconciliation.

Peace and Equality

Your true nature is non-confrontational and, being ruled by gentle Venus, the classic Libra stand is for non-violence. You would rather find a way to solve all wars by negotiation and to aim for an understanding of what divides people than resort to violence. Peace is Libra's domain and fairness and equality are Libra principles. You have to take action to defend your beliefs, but do so in a way that sets a good example for the rest of the world.

Style Ambassador

Your aesthetic sense and eye for symmetry means that you have a natural flair for what looks beautiful and appealing. Whether you make your surroundings more attractive to the eye at home or in the office, or you work in a career that's primarily about style, design or architecture, one of your Libra talents is to create beauty in the world. Share your affinity for good taste and loveliness.

Suave Sophistication

Your sign of Libra is renowned in zodiac terms as the definition of beauty. The women are feminine, curvy and elegant and the men stylish and handsome. Classic examples are Brigitte Bardot (28 September) and Roger Moore (14 October). Yours is the sign of old-school glamour, so sign up to style school and use your suave sophistication to make the right impression.

Unity And Oneness

You more than any other sign understand that opposites are an integral part of life, and wherever there's polarity, there's an opportunity for unity rather than division. Your analytical skills mean you're brilliant at finding the truth in each person's viewpoint or discerning the value in conflicting beliefs. Rather than take sides, you find a way to bring opposing forces together, to discover what they share in common rather than what distinguishes them as separate. Ultimately the Libra goal in life is to aim for unity and oneness, in self, others and the world.

Films, Books, Music

• • • • •

Films: *Breakfast at Tiffany's,* based on the novella by Truman Capote (30 September) or *Brokeback Mountain* director Ang Lee (5 October)

Books: *Hollywood Wives* by Jackie Collins (4 October) or *The Great Gatsby* by F. Scott Fitzgerald (24 September)

Music: A diverse range of musical genres, e.g. rock – Meat Loaf (27 September), rap – Eminem (17 October), jazz – Wynton Marsalis (18 October) or the iconic George Gershwin (26 September)

YOGA POSE:

Dancer: for flexibility and balance

TAROT CARD:

The Lovers

GIFTS TO BUY A LIBRA:

- a beautiful lamp or ornament
- champagne, chocs and flowers – the ultimate Libra birthday present
- an ice-cream maker
- a Japanese kimono
- a voucher for a spa or beauty treatment
- a stylish mirror
- a CD of classic jazz hits
- dinner at a top-class restaurant
- rose-scented perfume
- Star Gift – a chaise longue

Libra Celebrities Born On Your Birthday

SEPTEMBER

 23 John Coltrane, Ray Charles, Bruce Springsteen, Julio Iglesias

 24 F. Scott Fitzgerald, Jim Henson, Linda McCartney, Pedro Almodóvar, Jack Dee

 25 Ronnie Barker, Barbara Walters, Cheryl Tiegs, Michael Douglas, Mark Hamill,

Christopher Reeve, Michael Madsen,
Heather Locklear, Will Smith, Catherine
Zeta-Jones, Jessie Wallace, Declan
Donnelly, Jodie Kidd, Felicity Kendal, T.I.

 George Gershwin, Ricky Tomlinson,
Anne Robinson, Bryan Ferry, Olivia
Newton-John, Linda Hamilton, Serena
Williams

 Meat Loaf, Lil Wayne, Avril Lavigne,
Amma

 Brigitte Bardot, Naomi Watts, Dita von
Teese, Gwyneth Paltrow, Hilary Duff, Mira
Sorvino, Jennifer Rush

 Ian McShane, Kevin Durant, Zachary Levi

 Truman Capote, Barbara Knox, Rula
Lenska, Marion Cotillard, Monica Bellucci,
Omid Djalili, Martina Hingis, Angie
Dickinson

OCTOBER

1 Walter Matthau, Julie Andrews, Theresa May, Harry Hill, Keith Duffy, Brie Larson

2 Mahatma Gandhi, Groucho Marx, Donna Karan, Annie Leibovitz, Sting, Kelly Ripa, Ayumi Hamasaki

3 Tommy Lee, Clive Owen, Gwen Stefani, Neve Campbell, Ashlee Simpson, Vogue Williams, Alicia Vikander

4 Charlton Heston, Terence Conran, Susan Sarandon, Sarah Lancashire, Liev Schreiber, Anneka Rice, Alicia Silverstone, Akon, Dakota Johnson, Christoph Waltz, Jackie Collins

5 Bob Geldof, Kate Winslet, Nicky Hilton Rothschild, Nicola Roberts, Jesse Eisenberg, Guy Pearce

6 Melvyn Bragg, Britt Ekland, Linda Barker, Elisabeth Shue, Victoria Hervey

 7 Clive James, Yo-Yo Ma, Simon Cowell, Toni Braxton, Thom Yorke, Alesha Dixon, Jayne Torvill

 8 Jesse Jackson, Darrell Hammond, Paul Hogan, Chevy Chase, Sigourney Weaver, Matt Damon, Bruno Mars, Nick Cannon, Bella Thorne, Ardal O'Hanlon, Louise Hay

 9 Brian Blessed, John Lennon, Sharon Osbourne, David Cameron, P. J. Harvey, Nicky Byrne, Bella Hadid, Chris O'Dowd, Joe McFadden

 10 Thelonious Monk, Charles Dance, Chris Tarrant, Amanda Burton, Martin Kemp, Brett Favre, Mario Lopez

 11 Eleanor Roosevelt, Art Blakey, Daryl Hall, Dawn French, Luke Perry

12 Pavarotti, Angela Rippon, Les Dennis, Hugh Jackman, Katie Piper

13 Margaret Thatcher, Lenny Bruce, Paul Simon, Stephen Bayley, Kate Walsh, Paul Potts, Sacha Baron Cohen, Chelsy Davy, Marie Osmond, Kelly Preston

14 Roger Moore, Ralph Lauren, Cliff Richard, Steve Coogan, Usher, Lourdes Ciccone-Leon

15 P. G. Wodehouse, Sarah Ferguson, Stephen Tompkinson

16 Oscar Wilde, Angela Lansbury, Barry Corbin, Nico, Tim Robbins, Davina McCall, John Mayer, Shane Ward

17 Rita Hayworth, Cameron Mackintosh, Peter Stringfellow, Eminem, Felicity Jones, Mark Gatiss, Scarlett Moffatt

18 Wynton Marsalis, Martina Navratilova, Jean-Claude van Damme, Ne-Yo, Zac Efron, Freida Pinto,

 19 Kacey Ainsworth

 20 Danny Boyle, Tom Petty, Viggo Mortensen, Dannii Minogue, Snoop Dogg

 21 Judge Judy, Liliane Bettencourt, Dizzy Gillespie, Carrie Fisher, Kim Kardashian, Pelé, Amber Rose, Jade Jagger

 22 Derek Jacobi, Catherine Deneuve, Deepak Chopra, Jeff Goldblum, Spike Jonze

 23 Johnny Carson, Sarah Bernhardt, Anita Roddick, Ang Lee, Emilia Clarke, Cat Deeley

Q&A Section

• • • • •

Q. What is the difference between a Sun sign and a Star sign?

A. They are the same thing. The Sun spends one month in each of the twelve star signs every year, so if you were born on 1 January, you are a Sun Capricorn. In astronomy, the Sun is termed a star rather than a planet, which is why the two names are interchangeable. The term 'zodiac sign', too, means the same as Sun sign and Star sign and is another way of describing which one of the twelve star signs you are, e.g. Sun Capricorn.

Q. What does it mean if I'm born on the cusp?

A. Being born on the cusp means that you were born on a day when the Sun moves from one of the twelve zodiac signs into the next. However, the Sun doesn't change signs at the same time each year. Sometimes it can be a day earlier or a day later. In the celebrity birthday section of the book, names in brackets mean that this person's birthday falls into this category.

If you know your complete birth data, including the date, time and place you were born, you can find out definitively what Sun sign you are. You do this by either checking an ephemeris (a planetary table) or asking an astrologer. For example, if a baby were born on 20 January 2018, it would be Sun Capricorn if born before 03:09 GMT or Sun Aquarius if born after 03:09 GMT. A year earlier, the Sun left Capricorn a day earlier and entered Aquarius on 19 January 2017, at 21:24 GMT. Each year the time changes are slightly different.

Q. Has my sign of the zodiac changed since I was born?

A. Every now and again, the media talks about a new sign of the zodiac called Ophiuchus and about there now being thirteen signs. This means that you're unlikely to be the same Sun sign as you always thought you were.

This method is based on fixing the Sun's movement to the star constellations in the sky, and is called 'sidereal' astrology. It's used traditionally in India and other Asian countries.

The star constellations are merely namesakes for the twelve zodiac signs. In western astrology, the zodiac is divided into twelve equal parts that are in sync with the seasons. This method is called 'tropical' astrology. The star constellations and the zodiac signs aren't the same.

Astrology is based on a beautiful pattern of symmetry (see Additional Information) and it wouldn't be the same if a thirteenth sign were introduced into the pattern. So never fear, no one is going to have to say their star sign is Ophiuchus, a name nobody even knows how to pronounce!

Q. Is astrology still relevant to me if I was born in the southern hemisphere?

A. Yes, astrology is unquestionably relevant to you. Astrology's origins, however, were founded in the northern hemisphere, which is why the Spring Equinox coincides with the Sun's move into Aries, the first sign of the zodiac. In the southern hemisphere, the seasons are reversed. Babylonian, Egyptian and Greek and Roman astrology are the forebears of modern-day astrology, and all of these civilisations were located in the northern hemisphere.

* * * * *

Q. Should I read my Sun sign, Moon sign and Ascendant sign?

A. If you know your horoscope or you have drawn up an astrology wheel for the time of your birth, you will be aware that you are more than your Sun sign. The Sun is the most important star in the sky, however, because the other planets revolve around it, and your horoscope in the media is based on Sun signs. The Sun represents your essence, who you are striving to become throughout your lifetime.

The Sun, Moon and Ascendant together give you a broader impression of yourself as all three reveal further elements about your personality. If you know your Moon and Ascendant signs, you can read all three books to gain further insight into who you are. It's also a good idea to read the Sun sign book that relates to your partner, parents, children, best friends, even your boss for a better understanding of their characters too.

Q. Is astrology a mix of fate and free will?

A. Yes. Astrology is not causal, i.e. the planets don't cause things to happen in your life; instead, the two are interconnected, hence the saying 'As above, so below'. The symbolism of the planets' movements mirrors what's happening on earth and in your personal experience of life.

You can choose to sit back and let your life unfold, or you can decide the best course of action available to you. In this way, you are combining your fate and free will, and this is one of astrology's major purposes in life. A knowledge of astrology can help you live more authentically, and it offers you a fresh perspective on how best to make progress in your life.

Q. What does it mean if I don't identify with my Sun sign? Is there a reason for this?

A. The majority of people identify with their Sun sign, and it is thought that one route to fulfilment is to grow into your Sun sign. You do get the odd exception, however.

For example, a Pisces man was adamant that he wasn't at all romantic, mystical, creative or caring, all typical Pisces archetypes. It turned out he'd spent the whole of his adult life working in the oil industry and lived primarily on the sea. Neptune is one of Pisces' ruling planets and god of the sea and Pisces rules all liquids, including oil. There's the Pisces connection.

Q. What's the difference between astrology and astronomy?

A. Astrology means 'language of the stars', whereas astronomy means 'mapping of the stars'. Traditionally, they were considered one discipline, one form of study and they coexisted together for many hundreds of years. Since the dawn of the Scientific Age, however, they have split apart.

Astronomy is the scientific strand, calculating and logging the movement of the planets, whereas astrology is the interpretation of the movement of the stars. Astrology works on a symbolic and intuitive level to offer guidance and insight. It reunites you with a universal truth, a knowingness that can sometimes get lost in place of an objective, scientific truth. Both are of value.

Q. What is a cosmic marriage in astrology?

A. One of the classic indicators of a relationship that's a match made in heaven is the union of the Sun and Moon. When they fall close to each other in the same sign in the birth charts of you and your partner, this is called a cosmic marriage. In astrology, the Sun and Moon are the king and queen of the heavens; the Sun is a masculine energy, and the Moon a feminine energy. They represent the eternal cycle of day and night, yin and yang.

Q. What does the Saturn Return mean?

A. In traditional astrology, Saturn was the furthest planet from the Sun, representing boundaries and the end of the universe. Saturn is linked to karma and time, and represents authority, structure and responsibility. It takes Saturn twenty-nine to thirty years to make a complete cycle of the zodiac and return to the place where it was when you were born.

This is what people mean when they talk about their Saturn Return; it's the astrological coming of age. Turning thirty can be a soul-searching time, when you examine how far you've come in life and whether you're on the right track. It's a watershed moment, a reality check and a defining stage of adulthood. The decisions you make during your Saturn Return are crucial, whether they represent endings or new commitments. Either way, it's the start of an important stage in your life path.

Additional Information

• • • • •

The Symmetry of Astrology

There is a beautiful symmetry to the zodiac (see horoscope wheel). There are twelve zodiac signs, which can be divided into two sets of 'introvert' and 'extrovert' signs, four elements (fire, earth, air, water), three modes (cardinal, fixed, mutable) and six pairs of opposite signs.

One of the values of astrology is in bringing opposites together, showing how they complement each other and work together and, in so doing, restore unity. The horoscope wheel represents the cyclical nature of life.

Aries (*March 21–April 19*)

Taurus (*April 20–May 20*)

Gemini (*May 21–June 20*)

Cancer (*June 21–July 22*)

Leo (*July 23–August 22*)

Virgo (*August 23–September 22*)

Libra (*September 23–October 23*)

Scorpio (*October 24–November 22*)

Sagittarius (*November 23–December 21*)

Capricorn (*December 22–January 20*)

Aquarius (*January 21–February 18*)

Pisces (*February 19–March 20*)

ELEMENTS

There are four elements in astrology and three signs allocated to each. The elements are:

fire – Aries, Leo, Sagittarius
earth – Taurus, Virgo, Capricorn
air – Gemini, Libra, Aquarius
water – Cancer, Scorpio, Pisces

What each element represents:

Fire – fire blazes bright and fire types are inspirational, motivational, adventurous and love creativity and play

Earth – earth is grounding and solid, and earth rules money, security, practicality, the physical body and slow living

Air – air is intangible and vast and air rules thinking, ideas, social interaction, debate and questioning

Water – water is deep and healing and water rules feelings, intuition, quietness, relating, giving and sharing

MODES

There are three modes in astrology and four star signs allocated to each. The modes are:

cardinal – Aries, Cancer, Libra, Capricorn
fixed – Taurus, Leo, Scorpio, Aquarius
mutable – Gemini, Virgo, Sagittarius, Pisces

What each mode represents:

Cardinal – The first group represents the leaders of the zodiac, and these signs love to initiate and take action. Some say they're controlling.

Fixed – The middle group holds fast and stands the middle ground and acts as a stable, reliable companion. Some say they're stubborn.

Mutable – The last group is more willing to go with the flow and let life drift. They're more flexible and adaptable and often dual-natured. Some say they're all over the place.

INTROVERT AND EXTROVERT SIGNS/ OPPOSITE SIGNS

The introvert signs are the earth and water signs and the extrovert signs are the fire and air signs. Both sets oppose each other across the zodiac.

The 'introvert' earth and water oppositions are:

- Taurus – • Scorpio
- Cancer – • Capricorn
- Virgo – • Pisces

The 'extrovert' air and fire oppositions are:

- Aries – • Libra
- Gemini – • Sagittarius
- Leo – • Aquarius

THE HOUSES

The houses of the astrology wheel are an additional component to Sun sign horoscopes. The symmetry that is inherent within astrology remains, as the wheel is divided into twelve equal sections, called 'houses'. Each of the twelve houses is governed by one of the twelve zodiac signs.

There is an overlap in meaning as you move round the houses. Once you know the symbolism of all the star signs, it can be fleshed out further by learning about the areas of life represented by the twelve houses.

The houses provide more specific information if you choose to have a detailed birth chart reading.

This is based not only on your day of birth, which reveals your star sign, but also your time and place of birth. Here's the complete list of the meanings of the twelve houses and the zodiac sign they are ruled by:

1 – **Aries:** self, physical body, personal goals

2 – **Taurus:** money, possessions, values

3 – **Gemini:** communication, education, siblings, local neighbourhood

4 – **Cancer:** home, family, roots, the past, ancestry

5 – **Leo:** creativity, romance, entertainment, children, luck

6 – **Virgo:** work, routine, health, service

7 – **Libra:** relationships, the 'other', enemies, contracts

8 – **Scorpio:** joint finances, other people's resources, all things hidden and taboo

9 – **Sagittarius:** travel, study, philosophy, legal affairs, publishing, religion

10 – **Capricorn:** career, vocation, status, reputation

11 – **Aquarius:** friends, groups, networks, social responsibilities

12 – **Pisces:** retreat, sacrifice, spirituality

A GUIDE TO LOVE MATCHES

The star signs relate to each other in different ways depending on their essential nature. It can also be helpful to know the pattern they create across the zodiac. Here's a quick guide that relates to the chapter on Love Matches:

Two Peas In A Pod – the same star sign

Opposites Attract – star signs opposite each other

Soulmates – five or seven signs apart, and a traditional 'soulmate' connection

In Your Element – four signs apart, which means you share the same element

Squaring Up To Each Other – three signs apart, which means you share the same mode

Sexy Sextiles – two signs apart, which means you're both 'introverts' or 'extroverts'

Next Door Neighbours – one sign apart, different in nature but often share close connections